The Story of Milk

It Starts with Grass

Stacy Taus-Bolstad

Lerner Publications ◆ Minneapolis

Lerner Publications Company
An imprint of Lerner Publishing Group, Inc.
241 First Avenue North
Minneapolis, MN 55401 USA

For reading levels and more information, look up this title at www.lernerbooks.com.

Image credits: Image credits: Image Source/DigitalVision/Getty Images, p. 3; Xuanyu Han/Moment/Getty Images, pp. 5, 23 (cow); smereka/Shutterstock.com, p. 7; Mint Images/Getty Images, pp. 9, 23 (farmer); andhal/iStock/Getty Images, pp. 11, 23 (tank); kozmoat98/iStock/Getty Images, pp. 13, 23 (truck); Trinity Muller/Independent Picture Service, p. 15; Itsanan/Shutterstock.com, p. 17; Todd Strand/Independent Picture Service, p. 19; Ariel Skelley/DigitalVision/Getty Images, p. 21; skynesher/E+/Getty Images, p. 22. Cover: Alter_photo/iStock/Getty Images (milk); SunnyGraph/iStock/Getty Images (grass).

Main body text set in Mikado a Medium.
Typeface provided by HVD Fonts.

Editor: Alison Lorenz **Designer:** Lauren Cooper
Lerner team: Andrea Nelson

Library of Congress Cataloging-in-Publication Data

Names: Taus-Bolstad, Stacy, author.
Title: The story of milk : it starts with grass / Stacy Taus-Bolstad.
Description: Minneapolis : Lerner Publications, [2021] | Series: Step by step | Includes bibliographical references and index. | Audience: Ages 4–8 | Audience: Grades K–1 | Summary: "Simple, sequential sentences and colorful photos show readers how grass helps cows provide creamy, tasty milk"– Provided by publisher.
Identifiers: LCCN 2019045783 (print) | LCCN 2019045784 (ebook) | ISBN 9781541597280 (library binding) | ISBN 9781728401140 (ebook)
Subjects: LCSH: Milk–Juvenile literature. | Dairy cattle–Juvenile literature. | Dairying–Juvenile literature.
Classification: LCC SF239.5 .T385 2021 (print) | LCC SF239.5 (ebook) | DDC 636.2/142–dc23

LC record available at https://lccn.loc.gov/2019045783
LC ebook record available at https://lccn.loc.gov/2019045784

Manufactured in the United States of America
1-47832-48272-11/21/2019

Milk helps me grow.
Where does it come from?

A cow eats grass.

The cow makes milk.

A farmer milks
the cow.

A tank cools the milk.

A truck takes
the milk.

Machines clean the milk.

The milk is heated.

Machines put the milk in jugs.

People buy
the milk.

Yum!
Cold milk!

Picture Glossary

cow

farmer

tank

truck

Read More

Heos, Bridget. *From Milk to Cheese*. Mankato, MN: Amicus, 2018.

Koestler-Grack, Rachel A. *Grass to Milk*. Minneapolis: Bellwether Media, 2020.

McMullen, Gemma. *Milk and Dairy Products*. New York: AV2 by Weigl, 2017.

Index